Images of Modern America

JOHN F. KENNEDY
AT REST IN ARLINGTON

For two hours on the beautiful Sunday afternoon of March 3, 1963, John F. Kennedy (JFK) became a tourist in Washington, DC. He, along with old friend Charlie Bartlett, took a walk around the reflecting pool, toured the Aeronautics Building of the Smithsonian, and motored to Arlington National Cemetery to tour the Custis-Lee Mansion. Twenty-three-year-old Paul Fuqua, a mansion guide, stood with JFK in front of the house overlooking Washington. "I'd move the White House out here, the view is so beautiful," Fuqua told the president. "Yes," came JFK's reply, "I could stay here forever." In Arlington that day were Jean Austin; her husband, Larry; and their two boys. She wrote to Jacqueline Kennedy in June 1964 and sent the above photograph of JFK and Charlie Bartlett making their way toward the Custis-Lee Mansion. She wrote in part, "[We] were walking up the winding road between the Tomb of the Unknowns and the Custis-Lee Mansion when the two big black cars sped by us. . . . I jokingly remarked, there goes the president. We were so excited when we got to the house and saw that it actually was him." (Courtesy of JFK Library and Jean Austin.)

Images of Modern America

JOHN F. KENNEDY
AT REST IN ARLINGTON

R{\scriptsize AYMOND} S{\scriptsize INIBALDI}

ARCADIA
PUBLISHING

Copyright © 2020 by Raymond Sinibaldi
ISBN 978-1-4671-0403-6

Published by Arcadia Publishing
Charleston, South Carolina

Printed in the United States of America

Library of Congress Control Number: 2019954935

For all general information, please contact Arcadia Publishing:
Telephone 843-853-2070
Fax 843-853-0044
E-mail sales@arcadiapublishing.com
For customer service and orders:
Toll-Free 1-888-313-2665

Visit us on the Internet at www.arcadiapublishing.com

*For President and Mrs. John F. Kennedy, thank you for being
cauldrons of vision and hope. Your flame still burns.*

CONTENTS

Acknowledgments   6

Introduction   7

1.   The Days Dwindle down to a Precious Few   9

2.   The Eyes of Texas are upon You   27

3.   November 22, 1963   37

4.   Days of Anguish, Days of Splendor   47

5.   The Eternal Flame   61

6.   With Your Tiny Infants by Your Side   75

7.   With History the Final Judge of Our Deeds   85

About the Organization   95

ACKNOWLEDGMENTS

This book has been coming together for a long time and has been helped along by so many. To Krishna Shenoy, Mark Davies, Laurie Ivy, Lyndsey Richardson, and Stephen Fagin of the Sixth Floor Museum in Dealey Plaza, the professionalism, dedication, and exuberance that you bring to your mission is both infectious and inspiring. To Sara Pezzoni of the Special Collections at the Central Library from the University of Texas at Arlington, your passion and diligence are most appreciated. To my photographic consultants Rachael Adams, Lynda Fitzgerald, David Hickey, Margeaux Imperiale, Angela Sinibaldi, Elizabeth Sinibaldi-Rhodes, Josh Sinibaldi, Paula Sinibaldi, William Sinibaldi, and Julie Stoval, your thoughts, observations, and input were invaluable. To Carol Harding, Laura Howard, Matt Bumgardner, Lawrence H. Curtis, Azina Smart, Edward Crellin, Andrew Endres, Ron Cogswell, Lyndsey Tyler, Ann Longmore-Etheridge, and Donald Hughes, thank you for sharing your photographs and your compelling stories, all of which enhanced this project immensely. To Arlington National Cemetery historian Timothy Frank, thanks for opening so many doors. Caitrin Cunningham and Ryan Vied, working with you is a sheer joy. Last and certainly not least, to the staff at the John F. Kennedy Library—James Hill, Stacey Chandler, Abigail Malangone, Michelle DeMartion, Michael Desmond, Maryrose Grossman, and Heather Joines—thanks for always going above and beyond. White House photographers Robert Knudsen, Abbie Rowe, and Cecil Stoughton took the bulk of the photographs contained herein, and each one is marked with their last names. Others from unknown origin are marked JFK Library. Some come from the author's personal collection and are marked simply AC, while photographs taken by the author are marked RPS. Words attributed to individuals come from the following: *The Death of a President* by William Manchester, *Jackie's Newport* by Raymond Sinibaldi, *Five Days in November* by Clint Hill with Lisa McCubbin, John F. Kennedy Library oral histories, and the oral history project of the Sixth Floor Museum at Dealey Plaza. Quotes from President Kennedy's speeches come from the John F. Kennedy Library.

INTRODUCTION

It was 3:38 p.m. on a Friday afternoon, November 22, 1963. The flags in the nation's capital were flying at half-mast; the president of the United States was dead. In a stifling hot compartment aboard Air Force One, sitting on the tarmac of Love Field in Dallas, Texas, Lyndon Johnson was sworn in as the 36th president of the United States. Standing to his right was Lady Bird, his wife of 29 years; at his left was Jacqueline Kennedy, bedecked in a pink wool suit that bore the vestiges of the carnage that, two hours and thirty-eight minutes earlier, ended the life of her husband. The swearing-in took but 28 seconds, after which Jackie sat for a few minutes before returning to the rear of the plane; she wanted to be near her husband. She took a seat next to his coffin, and there she remained throughout the flight, never more than a matter of inches from his body.

Jacqueline Kennedy was transformed. In his painstakingly detailed chronology *Death of a President*, William Manchester wrote, "The new Jackie contrasted so sharply with the first lady they had known, that even the inner circle of Kennedy intimates were slow to grasp the extent of the volte-face . . . transformed by her vow that the full impact of the loss should be indelibly etched upon the national conscience." The manifestation of the new Jackie was continually revealed throughout the weekend and was first unveiled in the matter of "her dress," which was stained with remnants of brain tissue and the drying blood of her husband. Lady Bird Johnson was the first person to broach the matter. Sitting with her in her cabin, she gently suggested that someone help her change. She recalled Jackie's decline in her diary: "Oh no. Perhaps later . . . but not right now . . . with an element of fierceness—if a person that gentle, that dignified, can be said to have such a quality—she said 'I want them to see what they've done to Jack.' " Virtually all aboard the plane thought she should change, and a litany of men approached her, suggesting she do so. She held them all at bay, and when the rear cabin of Air Force One was opened in the dark of that November evening, Jackie emerged behind the coffin, revealing to the world "what they've done to Jack." It was this element of fierceness coupled with her vow that the full impact of the loss be seared into the national conscience that drove her.

The agonizing trip home took two hours and eighteen minutes during which plans for the president's funeral began to take shape in Jackie's mind. She remembered a conversation she'd had with him in November 1961. Returning from Arlington National Cemetery following the funeral of Anthony Biddle, Kennedy's ambassador to Spain, she asked him, "Where will we be buried when we die?" "Hyannis, I guess," came his casual reply, "We'll all be there." Jackie opined, "Well I don't think you should be buried in Hyannis, I think you should be buried in Arlington. You just belong to the whole country."

Talk on Air Force One inevitably moved toward the president's funeral and burial. The Kennedy family thought he would join his son Patrick in Brookline, Massachusetts, and aides Dave Powers, Ken O'Donnell, and Larry O'Brien (nicknamed "the Irish Mafia") could not conceive of the idea that he could lay anywhere but in Massachusetts soil. However, sitting in his office, Arlington superintendent John Metzler had a gut feeling and asked for his file on state funerals. And sitting next to her husband's coffin, Jackie thought he belonged to the whole country.

In Washington, Jackie's brother-in-law Sargent Shriver was meeting with JFK's protocol officer Angier Duke and Lt. Col. Paul Miller of the Military District of Washington, laying out plans for the president to lay in repose in the White House and in state beneath the Capitol Rotunda. Shriver, like Jackie, was thinking about Arlington, and he placed a call to Metzler asking if Roman Catholic services were permitted in a military cemetery and if children could be interred as well. Metzler's confirmation to Shriver that both were permissible confirmed his own gut feeling, and he directed his attention to which sites would be appropriate to bury the president of the United States.

Confusion reigned at Andrews Air Force Base when Air Force One came to rest at 6:05 p.m. A lift backed up to the plane's rear door. Within minutes and devoid of ceremony, a collection of secret servicemen, JFK aides, and an honor guard struggled to ease the burden of the 1,000-pound coffin, placing it in the rear of the waiting Navy ambulance. Jackie emerged, holding the hand of Robert Kennedy, and as the coffin was slid into place, she was assisted to the ground, where she briskly walked to the ambulance's rear door and climbed into its back seat. Once again, she was never more than a matter of inches from her husband's body.

An honor guard greeted them at Bethesda and escorted the body to the morgue for the autopsy while Jackie made her way to a suite on the 17th floor, where family and friends had gathered. It was in that suite where more specifics of the funeral began to emerge. The preference for a Massachusetts burial was reiterated by family and his closest aides. However, JFK's secretary of defense, Robert McNamara, felt differently and expressed that to Robert Kennedy. At his urging, McNamara spoke to Jackie. His words echoed Jackie's sentiment when he told her that he did not believe that President Kennedy should belong to just one part of the country. "A president, especially this president," he said "who has done so much for the nation's spiritual growth . . . enlarged our horizons and who has been martyred this way, belongs in a national environment."

Both John Metzler and Robert McNamara rose early on Saturday morning. And while widely circulated reports proclaimed a Boston burial, Metzler traversed his cemetery for suitable gravesites, and McNamara sat at his desk, educating himself on national cemeteries. McNamara's search led him to Metzler, and by the time Metzler received his call, he had chosen three possible sites. In the dreary dawn, the pair toured Arlington together. The hillside emerged as the obvious choice.

McNamara proceeded to the White House for a 10:00 a.m. mass in the East Room, after which he gathered up Robert Kennedy, Jean Kennedy Smith, Patricia Kennedy Lawford, and family friend and artist Bill Walton. They traveled to Arlington's hillside, now sloshy and muddied from persistent, chilling rain. The site spoke for itself, and to view it was to come to the realization that it was here where he belonged. Upon returning to the White House, Jean Smith told her sister-in-law, "We've found the most beautiful place," and Jackie knew it was time to decide. The contingent returned with her, adding two JFK friends, Lemoyne Billings and Jim Reed.

Jackie led the entourage up the hill. She stopped, an umbrella shielding her from the persistent, pelting rain. For 15 minutes, she stood silent, and then looking at Bill Walton, she nodded. Walton trudged the hillside and pointed to the spot where the grave should be, and John Metzler drove a stake into the ground. Months later, Jackie told William Manchester, "We went out and walked that hill and of course you knew that was where it should be."

On Monday, November 25, 1963, in regal splendor, John F. Kennedy was laid to rest "where he should be." As his coffin lay above his open grave, 50 Air Force fighters flew overhead, followed by Air Force One, which dipped its wing in a final salute. Taps were played, prayers were said, and then Jacqueline Kennedy, after lighting the eternal flame, took the hand of Robert Kennedy and left the hillside.

The centennial of John F. Kennedy's birth took place in May 2017, and by then, approximately a quarter of a billion people from all over the world had visited the Arlington hillside, where the full impact of the loss is still felt.

One

THE DAYS DWINDLE DOWN TO A PRECIOUS FEW

On August 7, 1963, Jacqueline Kennedy gave birth to Patrick Bouvier Kennedy. Six weeks premature, he was suffering from a respiratory condition known as Hyaline Membrane Disease. Young Patrick lived only 39 hours before succumbing to the condition, which today carries a 98 percent survival rate. By all accounts of family, friends, associates, and staff, the death of Patrick transformed the relationship of President Kennedy and Jackie Kennedy, bringing them closer than they had ever been.

September brought the 75th birthday celebration of the president's father, Joseph P. Kennedy, and the 10th wedding anniversary celebration of the president and first lady. In October, Jackie, accompanied by her sister Lee Radziwill, traveled to Greece, where they spent two weeks aboard the yacht *Christina*, owned by Greek shipping tycoon Aristotle Onassis. Meanwhile, the president twice traveled home to Massachusetts.

Included in those travels were visits with his dad in Hyannis Port and the grave of his son in Brookline. Presidential assistant and longtime friends Dave Powers and Kenny O'Donnell recalled those visits in *Johnny We Hardly Knew Ye*. At halftime of a Harvard/Columbia football game, President Kennedy, Dave, Kenny, and the Secret Service shook the press and traveled alone to Patrick's grave, whereupon JFK commented, "He seems so alone here." The following day was spent in Hyannis Port, and upon departure, President Kennedy said goodbye to his dad. Confined to a wheelchair since a stroke in 1961, he was wheeled onto the porch to welcome and say goodbye to his son. JFK customarily kissed him on the head before boarding. On this October day, walking toward the helicopter, he paused, turned around, and returned to kiss him a second time. Powers watched tears fill the president's eyes. "It was," he said, "as if he knew he was seeing him for the last time."

November's first two weekends found the first family enjoying their recently finished home in Atoka, Virginia, as the president prepared for what would be his first "campaign" trip for his 1964 reelection. It would entail four speeches in a day trip to Florida, followed by a two-day, five-city stop in Texas.

There were threats to assassinate JFK in both Tampa and Miami. The Secret Service, Tampa Police Office, Hillsboro County Sheriff's Office, and military personnel from Tampa's MacDill Air Force Base provided extra security on bridges, rooftops, and underpasses along JFK's Tampa motorcade, combating a threat to assassinate the president in Tampa.

On November 16, the Miami chief of police received a letter that read in part, "The Cuban Commandoes have the BOMBS ready for killindg [sp] JFK and Mayor KING HIGH either at the AIRPORT or at the Convention Hall." The FBI was not aware of the threat that was handled by the Miami police and the Secret Service. JFK's time in a motorcade was severely limited, and a helicopter was used instead. Air Force One left Florida at 9:20 p.m. with JFK safely aboard.

Texas awaited.

JFK's last summer began with a surprise party for his 46th birthday on May 29, 1963. Here, he and Jackie sort through his gifts while in the background Dave Powers (wearing glasses) and Kenny O'Donnell (sipping drink) look on. The party took place in the Navy Mess Hall at the White House. (Knudsen.)

The first family spent the first weekend in June at Camp David. JFK and Jackie had grown to enjoy Camp David, for it was there where they were afforded the privacy that they, especially Jackie, so valued. In this photograph, Paul Fay, a JFK war buddy and undersecretary of the Navy, shares a laugh with the president and his son at Camp David on a March 1963 visit. The three were watching Caroline riding her pony Macaroni. (Knudsen.)

JFK boards the memorial to the USS *Arizona*, where he laid a wreath on June 9. The memorial was built over the wreckage of the *Arizona*, now the grave of over 1,000 men who were killed when it was sunk during the Japanese sneak attack on Pearl Harbor on December 7, 1941, ushering America into World War II. JFK, who served in the Pacific during the war, was the first president to visit the memorial. (Knudsen.)

On June 10, JFK spoke at the commencement at American University in Washington, DC. He outlined his vision for world peace: "What kind of a peace do we seek . . . Not a Pax Americana enforced on the world by American weapons of war . . . genuine peace that enables . . . nations to grow and to hope and to build a better life for their children. . . . Not merely peace in our time but peace in all time." (Knudsen.)

In response to Alabama governor George Wallace's blocking the door to the University of Alabama to prevent the entrance of black students Vivian Malone and James Hood, JFK addressed the nation from the Oval Office. He said, "We face therefore a moral crisis as a country and as a people . . . It is time to act in the Congress, in your state and local legislative body and above all in our daily lives. . . . A great change is at hand and our task, our obligation is to make that revolution, that change peaceful and constructive for all. Those who do nothing are inviting shame as well as violence. Those who act boldly are recognizing right, as well as reality." That very same night, June 11, Medgar Evers was murdered in Mississippi, shot in the back in his driveway. Evers was interred in Arlington, and his family visited the White House. From left to right are Medgar's widow Myrlie Evers; daughter Reena; JFK; sons James and Darrell; and Medgar's brother Charles. (Both, Stoughton.)

In late June, JFK embarked on a 10-day tour through Germany, Ireland, England, and Italy. In Germany's West Berlin, he experienced a seminal moment in his presidency. In 1961, the Soviet Union constructed a wall to keep East Berliners from fleeing to West Berlin. He motorcaded through West Berlin (above) with West German chancellor Konrad Adenauer (waving) and West Berlin mayor Willy Brandt (center). Virtually every citizen of West Berlin viewed JFK during his three-day visit with one and a half million of them jamming the Rudolph Wilde Platz to hear him speak (below). At the wall, he delivered one of his most famous speeches: "2,000 years ago, the greatest boast was *civis romanus sum*. Today, in the world of freedom, the proudest boast is *Ich bin ein Berliner*." Assailing the tyranny of Communism, he closed, "All free men wherever they may live are citizens of Berlin, therefore, as a free man I take pride in the words *Ich bin ein Berliner*." (Both, Stoughton.)

From Germany, it was on to Ireland, where JFK spent what he called the three happiest days of his life. He visited the ancestral home of his cousin Mary Ryan (flowered dress, second from left) in Dunganstown County, Wexford. Also identified are Mary's daughters "Josie" (blue dress, far left) and Mary Ann (on JFK's left in pink dress). Mary Ann flew to Washington in November for JFK's funeral. Note the background banner. (Stoughton.)

In July, JFK spent a total of 15 days in Hyannis Port. It was rare indeed if JFK did not spend a part of every day on the sea, either aboard the *Honey Fitz*, the *Restuvus*, the *Marlin*, or at the tiller of a sailboat. Here, Caroline and her cousin Maria Shriver enjoy ice cream following a late July swim in Lewis Bay with JFK. They would often jump into the bay from the *Honey Fitz* to enjoy a swim. (Stoughton.)

Jackie Kennedy reads aboard the *Honey Fitz* as it cruises Lewis Bay off Hyannis Port. Caroline naps after an offshore swim with her dad and cousin Maria. It is the first weekend of August 1963, and Jackie is 34 weeks pregnant with a baby boy. Three days later, Patrick Bouvier Kennedy was delivered by emergency caesarian section at Otis Air Force Base in Mashpee, Massachusetts. Patrick lived only 39 hours. (Stoughton.)

Patrick was delivered by an emergency caesarian section at Otis Air Force Base and was immediately transferred to Boston Children's Hospital. JFK helicoptered back and forth between Jackie, Caroline, and John and Patrick. He was with Patrick when he died at 4:06 a.m. on August 9. Patrick was buried following a funeral mass at the residence of Richard Cardinal Cushing, Boston's archbishop. Jackie, too weak from surgery, was unable to attend. (AC.)

Taken on the day Jackie was released from the hospital, she boards Marine One, bound for their summer home on Squaw Island. It was Jackie's fifth pregnancy and the third baby she had lost. (Stoughton.)

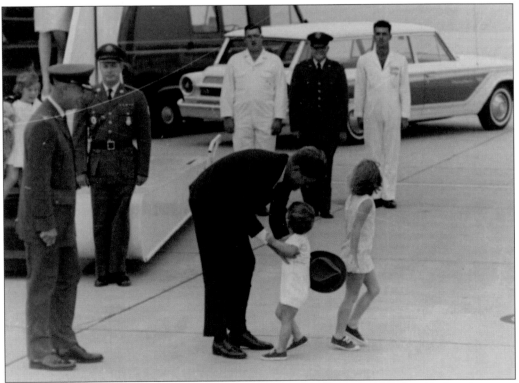

JFK is greeted by John Jr. upon his arrival at Otis Air Force Base on Cape Cod on Friday afternoon, August 23, 1963. Caroline had won the race to her daddy, capturing his first hug. It was a gloomy rainy weekend made even more so by the death of Patrick just two weeks earlier. Family friend William Walton said it was during this weekend that Jackie said to Jack, "The one thing I couldn't stand to lose is you." (Stoughton.)

On Labor Day weekend in 1963, CBS anchor Walter Cronkite taped an interview with President Kennedy on the lawn of Brambletyde, his summer home on Cape Cod. On Tuesday, September 3, the interview was aired on CBS News. Historical in its content regarding the growing conflict in Vietnam, it also marked the lengthening of *CBS Evening News* from a 15-minute broadcast to a half hour. ABC and NBC quickly followed suit. (Stoughton.)

September 7 marked the 75th birthday celebration for Joseph Kennedy. Singing was a staple of Kennedy family gatherings, and here, they sing to "Grampy Joe." JFK (in the chair) sang one of his favorites: "September Song." The song's most poignant line, "Oh the days dwindle down to a precious few. . . . And these few precious days, I'll spend with you." JFK had 74 precious days to live. (Stoughton.)

September 12 marked JFK and Jackie's 10th anniversary. They spent the weekend in Newport with family and close friends. While walking Bailey's Beach in Newport, father and son climbed into a rowboat, where they shared a tender moment. In the distance, friends Ben and Toni Bradlee walk the beach. President Kennedy had 66 precious days to live. (Stoughton.)

On September 30, the first family posed on the White House South Lawn with Caroline atop her pony Leprechaun, a gift from Ireland's president, Éamon de Valera. John Jr. is not too pleased as he holds onto his airplane. Enamored with flying machines, he often carried around a toy plane or helicopter. (Knudsen.)

In early October, JFK took a break from his presidential duties and strolled out to visit John and Caroline playing in their tree house. In a 1995 interview with Larry King, JFK Jr. said his first memory was teaching his dog Pushinka to slide down this slide. Pushinka was a gift from the Soviet Union and was the daughter of the first dog in space. (Knudsen.)

At halftime of a Harvard football game in October, JFK shook the press and visited Patrick's grave with Kenny O'Donnell and Dave Powers. "He seems so alone here," JFK commented. When Powers conveyed this story to Jackie on the plane back from Dallas, she commented to him, "I'll bring them together now." Ten days later, she did just that. (JFK Library.)

That night, JFK was the featured speaker before 6,000 Democrats gathered at Boston's Commonwealth Armory. The $100-a-plate dinner raised $750,000 for the Massachusetts state Democrats for the upcoming 1964 elections. Speaker of the House John McCormack (second from left) and Massachusetts governor Endicott Peabody (next to McCormack) shared the dais. Sen. Ted Kennedy is fourth from right. Five weeks later, McCormack eulogized President Kennedy in the Capitol Rotunda. (Stoughton.)

After twice kissing his father goodbye on October 20, 1963, JFK boarded Marine One to helicopter to Otis Air Force Base and Air Force One. With tears in his eyes, he said to Dave Powers, "He made all of this possible . . . now look at him." (Stoughton.)

President Kennedy's last visit to his home state came on October 26, when he spoke at the ground-breaking ceremonies for the Robert Frost Library at Amherst College in Amherst, Massachusetts. He said of Frost, "He was a very hard boiled man in his approach to life and in his desires for our country . . . he felt very strongly that the United States should be a country of power, of force . . . to use that power and force wisely." (Stoughton.)

JFK enjoys a Halloween laugh in the Oval Office with his son John while daughter Caroline strikes a somber, scary pose as the witch with her black cat. (Stoughton.)

The Kennedy family home in Atoka, Virginia, was named Wexford in honor of Wexford County, Ireland, from where the president's ancestors immigrated. The home was finished in October. Wexford provided privacy and a place for Jackie to partake in her passion for riding. The family spent only two weekends there. In the photograph at left, John gets a hug from mom as he pauses from play. He loved to play soldier, and during those times, his mom would teach him to salute. Jackie often described his salute as "sort of droopy." However, the Secret Service and some military aides began assisting in his tutelage. In the photograph below, JFK chats with John on his bike while Caroline swings on the swing set. Jackie spent little time there following the president's death and sold it within a year. (Both, Stoughton.)

The president made two official visits to Arlington National Cemetery in 1963. The first came on Memorial Day, May 30 (right), where he confers with Maj. Gen. Paul Gavan, commanding general of the Military District of Washington, before the ceremonies are about to begin. The second was Veteran's Day, just 11 days before his death. He laid a wreath at the Tomb of the Unknowns. In the photograph below, John greets his dad after the ceremonies. The younger Kennedy actually stole the show. Fascinated with the stoic solemnity of the soldiers, he walked up to one, and with his hands behind his back in an inspection-type pose, he stood at his feet and stared up at him. Exactly two weeks later, on November 25, JFK was laid to rest in Arlington. The next time John Jr. visited Arlington, it was to visit his father's grave. (Right, Knudsen; below, Stoughton.)

On November 13, the Black Watch, Great Britain's Royal Highland Regiment, performed on the White House South Lawn. Under the direction of Jackie Kennedy, 1,700 students who were served by the United Givers Fund (precursor to the United Way) were invited to the event. The Black Watch was founded in 1739 under King George II. In welcoming them, JFK told the commander, Maj. Wingate Gray (seen above left), "We are proud to have them here . . . because they are a Scottish Regiment, and that green and misty country has sent hundreds and thousands of Scottish men and women to the United States and they have been among our finest citizens." Flying back on Air Force One from Dallas, sitting next to her husband's coffin, Jackie, recalling JFK's love for the Black Watch, made the decision to include them in the president's funeral. (Both, Knudsen.)

President Kennedy's final weekend was spent in Florida at his parent's Palm Beach home. On Saturday, November 16, he visited Cape Canaveral for an inspection and update on the status of the Saturn rocket development. In the photograph above, at Pad B, Complex 37, JFK (far right) is briefed by Dr. Wernher Von Braun. It was then on to the deck of the USS *Observation Island* (right) to view a launch demonstration of the Polaris A-2 missile from the submarine the USS *Andrew Jackson*. Here, he is speaking to the crew of the *Jackson*. Coming aboard, he received a windbreaker from both crews, which he is wearing. From left to right are Rear Adm. Vernon L. Lowrance; captain of the *Observation Island*, Roderick Middleton (partially hidden); JFK; and naval aide Capt. Tazewell T. Shepard. (Above, Stoughton; right, Knudsen.)

The Weather
Tampa Bay Forecast—Fair and Mild
with East to Southeast Winds 12-22 MPH.
High Today Near 80, Low 57. (National
Weather Map, Page 8-C).

THE TAMPA TRIBUNE

PINELLAS

Pinellas
Edition

69TH YEAR—No. 322   THREE SECTIONS — 40 PAGES   TAMPA, FLORIDA, MONDAY NOVEMBER 18, 1963   PRICE TEN CENTS
7 Days Home Delivery 56 Cents

Mr. President

Kennedy To Make Three Speeches in Tampa Today

Throngs Expected To Greet President

By PAUL WILDER
Tribune Staff Writer

Tampa was ready today for the first visit of a president in the city's history.

Hundreds of people were involved in preparation of the myriad details of the four-hour visit of President John F. Kennedy.

Thousands will be able to see him in person, if only briefly, as he rides in fast-moving motorcades along Dale Mabry, Grand Central, Franklin Street and Cass Street between 2 and 4 p.m. this afternoon.

He'll Be on Television

Many more thousands will see him on television. WFLA-TV will begin telecasting at 1:30 p.m. as he arrives at Loper Field by helicopter from Mac-Dill Air Force Base. WTVT will telecast at 1:45 as the President speaks on the 50th anniversary of commercial aviation. A

Map Showing Streets Pres. Kennedy Will Pass Through is on Page 1-B

wrapup of the day's events will be presented on WFLA-TV in a special telecast at 7 p.m.

Some 8,000 to 10,000 persons were expected to cram into Al Lopez Field, where the front

It is widely accepted that President Kennedy's trip to Texas was the unofficial kickoff for his 1964 reelection campaign. However, the fact is, that actually occurred on Monday, November 18 in Florida. In the 1960 election, he lost the state of Florida, and its 10 electoral votes by three percent of the vote. One area where he did not show well was Pinellas County, which includes parts of St. Petersburg and Tampa. (AC.)

He made three speeches in the Tampa area before ending the day with a speech in Miami. He motorcaded through downtown Tampa on a street that today is called Kennedy Boulevard. A monument to President Kennedy was dedicated on May 30, 1966, and still stands on the Kennedy Boulevard side on the University of Tampa campus, as seen here. The president's precious days were down to four. (RPS.)

Two

THE EYES OF TEXAS
ARE UPON YOU

On Thursday morning, November 21, 1963, President Kennedy wrapped up a five-minute meeting, left the Oval Office, went upstairs to the living quarters, and tapped on Jackie's bedroom door. Her hairdresser, Kenneth, was adding his last-minute touches. The helicopter was on the lawn. Kenneth finished, and Jackie made her way downstairs, where her husband and son were waiting. He would remember thinking that he had never seen them so happy.

A vigorous three-pronged campaign swing would take them to San Antonio, Houston, Fort Worth, Dallas, and Austin, then a respite at the LBJ Ranch and back to the White House on Sunday. The purpose was to patch up a schism in Texas's Democrat party between the factions of Lyndon Johnson and Sen. Ralph Yarbrough, which had Gov. John Connolly right in the middle. The others were to see as many voters as possible and, of course, to fundraise. Five cities and five speeches were to happen in about 36 hours. They were scheduled to ride in a dozen open motorcades through the streets of five Texas cities, and it was estimated that one million people would see the president and his first lady, approximately 10 percent of the entire population of Texas.

In 1960, JFK carried Texas and its 24 electoral votes by a slim popular vote margin of two percent—a margin that could be attributed to the presence of former Texas senator Lyndon Johnson on the ticket. Texas was essential to his 1964 hopes, and the split in the state's Democratic party as well as the civil rights legislation that JFK had sent to Congress were causes for concern in segregated Texas. There was trepidation on behalf of many in the Kennedy White House regarding the trip to Texas. A trepidation that was minimized by the throngs that welcomed them off Air Force One and lined each motorcade route cheering wildly for "Jack and Jackie."

There was a space theme to the president's speeches, which began in San Antonio, moved to his testimonial for Congressman Albert Thomas in Houston, and to his speech outside Fort Worth's Hotel Texas on the morning he died. Referring to the conquest of "space, the new sea," he said it is "an area where the United States should be second to none." His undelivered speeches at both the Dallas Trade Mart and at the governor's mansion in Austin each contained the phrase, "The United States of America has no intention of finishing second in outer space."

San Antonio was the first stop. When the doors swung open, the 20,000-plus gathered began chanting, "Jackie!" The protocol calls for the president to always be the first one off the plane; however, hearing the crowd, JFK stepped back to make way for his wife. He would do this for the entire Texas trip. They were greeted by San Antonio mayor Walter McAllister and his wife, Edith. (Stoughton.)

In dedicating the Aerospace Medical Health Center in San Antonio, JFK said that the United States had "tossed its cap over the wall of space and had no choice but to follow it." He then ventured to the center and spoke with four Navy volunteers in a hyperbaric oxygen chamber to learn its effects on humans. JFK asked Dr. Bill Welch if this work might improve oxygen chambers for premature babies. (Stoughton.)

The *San Antonio Light* wrote of the "wildly enthusiastic greeting" the Kennedys received. School was out for the day, and over 125,000 people lined the motorcade route. Placards were waved that read, "Welcome JFK," "Bienvenido Mr. President," and one even implored Jackie to "Come Waterski in Texas." (Stoughton.)

It was around 4:30 Texas time when Air Force One landed at Houston International Airport. Once again, Jackie led the way off the plane and was greeted by 10,000 people and the University of Houston Marching Band playing "The Marines' Hymn." The motorcade route was lined by 200,000 people, and another throng awaited them outside the Rice Hotel. (Stoughton.)

That evening, Council 60 of the League of United Latin American Citizens (LULAC) was holding its state director's ball at the Rice Hotel. The Secret Service had told them that the president and first lady would stop by and wave hello to the gathering. They not only got a few words from JFK, but he introduced Jackie, who addressed them in Spanish, bringing down the house. (Stoughton.)

It was then on to the Houston Coliseum and a testimonial dinner for Congressman Albert Thomas. Thomas had been an ardent supporter of JFK's space program. What Jackie remembered of this event was JFK's conclusion, quoting the Book of Acts: "Your old men will dream dreams, your young men will see visions. . . . And where there is no vision the people perish. Albert Thomas is old enough to dream dreams and young enough to see visions." (Stoughton.)

It was approaching midnight when Air Force One landed in Fort Worth, yet despite the late hour, 10,000 people greeted JFK and Jackie. In the line, two Catholic schoolboys received a kiss on the head from the first lady and a pat from President Kennedy. As they came upon the city (note top of newspaper), they noticed that the tallest buildings had been illuminated in a tribute to them. (*Fort Worth Star-Telegram* Collection, Special Collections, the University of Texas at Arlington Libraries.)

Eighteen-year-old Doris Giddens was in the front row in the parking lot outside Fort Worth's Hotel Texas. Recalling the day, she remembered thinking, "He's a good looking man for an old man." There was intense excitement in the crowd, and Giddens was struck by his "auburn hair and the sun shone behind him and his hair glowed. . . . He had so much energy, your eyes went right to him." (Stoughton.)

Ruth Carter Johnson (left) and Lucile Weiner (right) deliver Picasso's *Angry Owl* to Suite 850 at Hotel Texas. Local devotees of fine art put together an exhibit for the first couple. Arriving late Thursday night, it went unnoticed until Friday morning after the chamber of commerce breakfast. It turned out to be the final moments of relaxation and serenity that JFK and Jackie would spend together, and they called Ruth Johnson to thank her. (*Fort Worth Star-Telegram* Collection, Special Collections, the University of Texas at Arlington Libraries.)

The crowd erupted in cheers when Jackie arrived at breakfast. One reporter commented that she had never seen women dressed up and in heels stand on a chair. But they did to get a better look at Jackie. JFK opened his speech with, "Two years ago I introduced myself in Paris by saying I was the man who had accompanied Mrs. Kennedy to Paris. I'm getting somewhat that same sensation as I travel around Texas." (Stoughton.)

Jackie was invigorated by the hour they spent upstairs before their departure for Dallas, and she said to JFK, "Jack, it's easy campaigning when your president, I'll go anywhere with you." Jumping on the opportunity, he replied, "How about California in two weeks?" Both he and Ken O'Donnell were delighted that she agreed. They then left for a motorcade to Carswell Air Force Base. JFK is standing in the white convertible in front of city hall. (Stoughton.)

President and Mrs. Kennedy, with Governor Connolly, travel along the motorcade route for the 35-minute ride to Carswell Air Force Base. Schools in Fort Worth were closed for the day, and the motorcade was greeted by high school marching bands and thousands of enthusiastic Fort Worth citizens. (*Fort Worth Star-Telegram* Collection, Special Collections, the University of Texas at Arlington Libraries.)

Before leaving the Hotel Texas, JFK held an impromptu press conference in its lobby. Standing against a desk was five-year-old Olivia Duke. As the crowd surged, she was in danger of being crushed when a hotel clerk rescued her and placed her standing upon a desk five feet behind the president. Fifty-four years later, choking back tears, Duke recalled that morning, and she said, "I remember his essence, and I have carried his essence with me my whole life." At Carswell Air Force Base, JFK and Jackie worked the line, shaking hands and signing autographs. As they came toward the end of the line, JFK signs for a fan while Jackie signs as well, right behind him. This may well be the last autograph signed by President Kennedy because within minutes, they broke from the line to board Air Force One for Dallas. (Both, *Fort Worth Star-Telegram* Collection, Special Collections, the University of Texas at Arlington Libraries.)

The incredible reception President and Mrs. Kennedy received throughout Texas, particularly in Fort Worth and even Dallas itself, exceeded any and all expectations. Congressman James Wright (second from right in both photographs) was "overcome with joy . . . to have the President of the United States talking with my constituents, my folks." The morning had been, in his words, one of "ebullient joy." These photographs capture a tender moment shared by Jackie and JFK. As they broke from the crowd, they walked hand in hand for about 50 feet and were captured in this rare public display of affection. (Both, *Fort Worth Star-Telegram* Collection, Special Collections, the University of Texas at Arlington Libraries.)

President Kennedy boards Air Force One with Jackie in front of him and Dave Powers to his left. Cornelia Friedman, the wife of Fort Worth's mayor Bayard Friedman, shared the head table with President and Mrs. Kennedy at the chamber of commerce Hotel Texas breakfast and was present when he departed Carswell Air Force Base. She watched JFK turn and wave goodbye before boarding Air Force One for Dallas. Turning to her husband, she said, "I hope they behave themselves in Dallas today." John Fitzgerald Kennedy, the nation's 35th president, had 95 precious minutes to live. Fifty years later, the surviving members of JFK's head table that Friday morning gathered to commemorate the event. Julian Read, Governor Connolly's press secretary, toasted President Kennedy. Cornelia Friedman recalled, "None of us had even voted for Kennedy but by the end of the day we were, just like everybody else, totally captivated." (*Fort Worth Star-Telegram* Collection, Special Collections, the University of Texas at Arlington Libraries.)

Three

November 22, 1963

Dallas was a cause for deeper concern. Not only had it had gone to Richard Nixon with 62 percent of the vote in 1960, but it had also twice exhibited open hostility to members of Kennedy's administration. During the 1960 campaign, Lyndon Johnson (a Texas favorite son) and his wife, Lady Bird, were "hissed at and spat upon," as it took 45 minutes to navigate 50 yards through a hostile crowd. Just one month earlier, in October 1963, Kennedy's United Nations ambassador Adlai Stevenson had been spat upon and struck during an anti-United Nations, anti-administration demonstration. Dallas was a cauldron of hard-right political thought and activism, causing concern among Kennedy advisors regarding his visit.

On Friday morning, November 22, posters were distributed throughout parts of the city, which read, "Wanted for Treason" under two photographs of JFK. Among his "crimes" were "turning over US sovereignty to the communist-controlled United Nations, illegally invading a sovereign state with federal troops (Alabama and Mississippi) and giving support and encouragement to the communist-inspired race riots." The *Dallas Morning Herald* ran a full-page advertisement purchased by the American Fact Finding Committee and financed by Texas oil mogul H.L. Hunt. Under the headline "Welcome Mr. Kennedy," 12 questions were asked of the president, all regarding their perception that he was soft on communism. It was this advertisement that initiated his quip to Jackie before leaving suite 850 in Fort Worth's Hotel Texas: "We're heading into nut country."

Despite all the trepidation and anxiety about Dallas, things could not have gone better. Congressman Wright stated in his oral interview for the Sixth Floor Museum, "I wondered about Dallas . . . I needn't had." He added he was "overjoyed by the marvelously hospitable turnout of people all the way from Love Field . . . through the city streets." Dallas was "wonderful, gracious, warm." In a 1991 C-Span interview, Governor Connolly recalled the Dallas crowd being "extremely enthusiastic, warm, excited . . . exuberant." Kenny O'Donnell wrote that the "throngs of people jamming the streets and hanging out of windows were all smiling, waving and shouting excitedly. The steady roar of their cheering was deafening. It was by far the greatest, and most emotionally happy crowd we had ever seen in Texas." Riding just behind the president's car, O'Donnell turned to Dave Powers and said, "This is one state we're going to carry easily." The limousine made a right-hand turn onto Houston Street and was moving towards the Texas School Book Depository. Nellie Connolly turned to the president and said, "You can't say Dallas doesn't love you Mr. President," to which he replied, "No, no you can't." They then turned left onto Elm Street, and the "happiest" day in the life of Congressman James Wright turned into the "saddest."

Lost in the horror of JFK's assassination was the remarkable reception he and Jackie received in the Dallas motorcade.

And in Dealey Plaza stood six-year-old Jeff Franzen. He recalled watching the motorcade 51 years later for the Sixth Floor Museum Oral History Project: "Jackie was looking at us . . . I saw a big spray up in the air . . . I assumed it was confetti . . . [because] I thought the shots were firecrackers."

As she had done in San Antonio, Houston, and Fort Worth, Jackie leads her husband off Air Force One to the cheering throng gathered at Love Field in Dallas. (Stoughton.)

In this rarely seen photograph taken from inside Air Force One, JFK and Jackie are seen at the end of the receiving line at Love Field. The presidential limousine is seen off to the right. Jackie stands behind JFK and Gov. John Connolly (who has his arm around JFK). Bottom left, LBJ has his arm around Lady Bird who is chatting with Dallas mayor Earle Cabell and his wife, "Birdie." (JFK Library.)

Kathy Atkinson was 12 years old and in the crowd along the fence at Love Field. JFK made his way toward her, but the crowd surged, and she was pinned on the ground. She stuck her hand up and heard a voice say, "Let her through," and she felt a hand in hers lifting her—"The next thing I knew, I was looking in JFK's eyes." (Stoughton.)

JFK and Jackie get situated in the back seat of the limousine as they get ready to depart Love Field and motorcade through downtown Dallas to the Trade Mart luncheon and speech. The chef at the Trade Mart wanted to cook the biggest, juiciest steak in Texas. However, he was instructed by the Secret Service to cook all the 2,000 steaks for the luncheon, and they would select one for the president to eat. (JFK Library.)

Perched on a balcony of the Adolphus Hotel on Main Street, *Dallas Times Herald* photographer Bill Beal captured both the exuberance of the reception and the vulnerability of the president riding in an open convertible through the throngs. The crowd continuously surged on the president's side, causing driver Will Greer to move to the left, bringing Jackie ever closer to the crowd. Clint Hill (wearing sunglasses above and just to the left of Jackie's pillbox hat in the below) was continually jumping back and forth from the Secret Service car to the back bumper of the limousine. (Both photographs by Bill Beal, *Dallas Times Herald* Collection/the Sixth Floor Museum at Dealey Plaza.)

These photographs were taken virtually simultaneously from opposite sides of Houston Street, within seconds after the limousine made the turn into Dealey Plaza from Main Street. Standing on the corner of Houston and Elm Streets, approximately 100 feet in front of them, just below the Texas School Book Depository, was 11-year-old Toni Glover. "I was fascinated with the Kennedys," she recalled, and she noticed that JFK and Jackie had turned toward each other. "They had a couple moment . . . and it made me smile," she remembered, and as the limousine rolled past her and made the turn on to Elm Street, she said to herself, "This is the greatest moment of my life." JKF had precious few seconds remaining. (Above, Jay Skaggs Collection/the Sixth Floor Museum at Dealey Plaza; below, Phil Willis Collection/the Sixth Floor Museum at Dealey Plaza.)

The car turned left onto Elm Street and was seconds away from the safety of the underpass. Phil Willis testified before the Warren Commission that the first "shot caused me to squeeze the camera shutter, and I got a picture of the President as he was hit." To the right of the Stemmons sign, Abraham Zapruder is seen filming, and Clint Hill (right of motorcycle on front of running board) has heard a shot and is scanning the president's vehicle. Within five seconds, Hill will be on the back of the vehicle, pushing Jackie back down in the back seat. Agent Paul Landis (behind Hill) was "looking right at the president and heard the third shot. I saw his head explode . . . blood and flesh fly . . . I knew they got him." Below, chaos reigns outside the Parkland Hospital emergency room. (Above, Phil Willis Collection/the Sixth Floor Museum at Dealey Plaza; below, *Fort Worth Star-Telegram* Collection, Special Collections, the University of Texas at Arlington Libraries.)

President Kennedy arrived at Parkland Hospital with a fatal gunshot wound to the brain. Had he been anyone but the president, he would have been declared dead on arrival; however, his heart was still beating. The futile attempt to resuscitate ended 22 minutes after his arrival when he was formally declared dead by Dr. Kemp Clark. Outside Parkland, four Dallas policemen watch as Secret Service agents wash the presidents' limousine. An uproar ensued inside of Parkland regarding legal jurisdiction over the president's autopsy. It did not help the ensuing investigations that the Secret Service had cleansed a crime scene. Jackie ultimately left Parkland Hospital with the body of her husband. The morning's ebullient joy had morphed into "unutterable pathos . . . unspeakable sadness." Below, Jackie follows the coffin of JFK onto Air Force One. (Above, JFK Library; below, Stoughton.)

This is a rarely seen shot of President Kennedy's coffin being carried aboard Air Force One by his aides and Secret Servicemen. Taken from the cabin of Air Force Two, Jackie is in pink at the foot of the stairs. She sat by his coffin the entire trip back to Washington, DC, with Dave Powers and Kenny O'Donnell and began planning her husband's funeral. (JFK Library.)

JFK's coffin is placed in a Navy ambulance bound for Bethesda Naval Hospital and an autopsy. In the back of the truck are, from left to right, Robert Kennedy (who had met the plane upon arrival and entered the plane's front entrance), Jackie, Clint Hill, and Larry O'Brien. (Stoughton.)

Texas congressman Jim Wright, one of the key planners of JFK's visit to Fort Worth, traveled with him on Air Force One from Fort Worth and rode in the Dallas motorcade. Like virtually everyone present, he was thrilled at the tremendous reception JFK and Jackie received in Dallas. Speaking about that tragic day 33 years later, he captured the incongruity of the day's events. The morning began with "such ebullient joy" and ended in "unutterable pathos and unspeakable sadness." Nothing captures that sentiment as clearly as these two photographs taken less than three hours apart. Above left, JFK and Jackie have just deplaned at Dallas's Love Field and are on their way to greet the people in the crowd. Above right, Jackie stands with Lyndon Johnson in the cabin of Air Force One as he is sworn in. Her husband's coffin was sitting in the rear cabin of the plane. (Both, Stoughton.)

Another testimony to the day's extremes was the front page of the *Dallas Times Herald*. The photograph at left is of the layout editor's copy for the front page of the afternoon's edition on November 22. "JFK Takes City By Storm," "Dallas Greets President," "Crowds Cheer Wildly For JFK," and "Jackie Sparkles, Ladybird Too" blared his version of the day's events—a chronology of the morning of "ebullient joy." Six seconds on Elm Street turned it all to horror. The edition, which hit the streets, was mired in "unutterable pathos . . . unspeakable sadness" (Left, the Sixth Floor Museum; below, Special Collections, the University of Texas at Arlington Libraries.)

Four

DAYS OF ANGUISH, DAYS OF SPLENDOR

A generation of baby boomers were the children of John F. Kennedy's New Frontier, and they sat riveted to their televisions throughout the weekend, watching their president honored, mourned, and laid to rest. New words were added to their lexicon as they learned of a catafalque, a cortege, a cordon, a caisson, and a caparisoned horse. With each term came an indelible image marking them for a lifetime.

Already on alert due to the illness of the nation's 31st president Herbert Hoover, Washington's Military District began instant preparation for JFK's state funeral. He would lay in repose in the East Room of the White House, which was draped in black—a tradition that dated back to 1841 and William Henry Harrison, the first president to die in office. A riderless caparisoned horse with boots backward in the stirrups of his empty saddle, signifying the loss of a leader, followed his caisson through Washington's streets in traditions set by the deaths of Zachary Taylor and Abraham Lincoln. JFK would lie in state in the Capitol Rotunda nearly a century after Lincoln, who was the first president to do so. And his coffin would lay upon the Lincoln Catafalque, as Presidents Lincoln, Garfield, McKinley, Harding, and Taft had done before him. His funeral procession marched up Pennsylvania Avenue just as seven preceding presidents who died in office, and he would do so upon the caisson that bore Franklin Roosevelt in 1945. With all the pageantry of honor guards, military units, and military bands steeped in tradition, dating all the way back to George Washington and beyond, John F. Kennedy was laid to rest. And from the far reaches of the earth, an outpouring of sorrow and grief, the likes of which the world had never seen, descended upon the nation's capital, expressed in thought, word, and deed.

At the center of it all was Jacqueline Kennedy, the 34-year-old widow, and their two young children. Caroline Kennedy turned six years old two days after her father was buried, and John F. Kennedy Jr. saluted his father's coffin on his third birthday.

In her grief, Jacqueline Kennedy was transformed from the first lady of the United States to a world icon, venerated for her courage, strength, grace, and dignity. In those heart-wrenching days of anguish and splendor, Jacqueline Kennedy led her country, and as it was written in Kansas, "In the eyes of her countrymen, her darkest hour has been her finest."

Jackie brings her husband home to the White House just after 4:00 a.m. the morning of November 23, 1963. Still wearing her blood-stained suit, she is accompanied by Robert Kennedy to her left. Behind them are Eunice Kennedy Shriver (left) and her husband, Sargent Shriver; Defense Secretary Robert McNamara (wearing glasses); Ethel Kennedy; JFK's naval aide, Capt. Tazewell Shepard (in the white hat); and behind him, Dave Powers. (Stoughton.)

On the Concord Green, in the shadow of the Minute Man statue in Concord, Massachusetts, the Concord Battery gathered at dawn to salute the fallen president. America's oldest independent horse-drawn cannon company was established in 1804 and had fired its cannons in tribute to assassinated Presidents Lincoln, Garfield, and McKinley. Every US military establishment in the world fired cannons every half hour from sunrise to sunset the day after JFK was killed. (JFK Library.)

On Saturday, November 23, 1963, John F. Kennedy lay in state in the East Room of the White House. At 10:00 a.m., a mass was celebrated as the Kennedy family and close friends gathered. Sargent Shriver observed on Jackie "a mask of agony" and Caroline Kennedy "with intelligence, compassion and love trying to comfort her mother." Jackie spent most of the day on Saturday in the family quarters at the White House, making burial/funeral plans. She left only to visit Arlington to place her stamp of approval on the burial site. Throughout the day in the East Room, various Kennedys played host as Kennedy Appointees, the cabinet, White House staffers, the Supreme Court, Congress, governors, dignitaries, and diplomats paid their respects. Among them were Presidents Truman and Eisenhower and Chief Justice Earl Warren and his wife, Elisabeth, seen below. (Above, Rowe; below, JFK Library.)

On Sunday, Jackie made her first public appearance since her return from Dallas. Following mass, the East Room was cleared, and the coffin was opened, where Jackie placed letters written by her and Caroline and a drawing done by JFK Jr. She also placed with him gold-inlaid cuff links she gave him on their first anniversary and a custom carved scrimshaw of the presidential seal she gave him the previous Christmas. Bobby placed with his brother his PT-109 tie clasp and rosary beads Ethel gave him when they were married. Clint Hill wrote, "The sight and sounds of their agony is something I will never forget." In these two photographs, Jackie and her children follow the coffin out of the White House and watch it placed upon the caisson. John asked why the soldiers moved so slow, to which Jackie replied, "Because they are so sad." (Left, Stoughton; below, JFK Library.)

Lawrence Curtis was a student at Duke University who drove from Durham, North Carolina, to Washington and became one of the million people who witnessed JFK's funeral. Early Monday morning, he took this photograph of the open grave, which Jackie had selected two days earlier in a bitterly cold November rain. The grave lay on the same axis point as the Custis-Lee Mansion and the Lincoln Memorial. (Lawrence H. Curtis 2019.)

The caisson, which also bore Franklin Delano Roosevelt, carries JFK up Constitution Avenue to lie in state in the Capitol Rotunda. Elected to a fourth term in failing health in 1944, FDR determined that a state funeral with World War II raging would be inappropriate. Thus, the only public viewing took place when his caisson bore him from the White House to the train station for transport to Hyde Park, New York, for burial. (Stoughton.)

Waiting at the corner of Constitution Avenue and First Street was 17-year-old Donald Hughes, who, like countless millions of young people, was deeply moved by the assassination of President Kennedy. As senior class president and yearbook photographer, Hughes felt a "duty" to capture the events. What he captured was the heartbreak and sadness of the American people as well. Above, two soldiers of the cordon salute as their commander in chief approaches, and in the photograph below, Hughes captured a most poignant historical moment as John John peers out at mourners and Caroline sits perched in the middle seat with Lady Bird Johnson, blocking her Uncle Bobby from camera's view. Jackie and Lyndon B. Johnson were in the back seat. The grief, sadness, and sorrow are etched on the faces of all. Hughes's photographs were displayed in the Sixth Floor Museum exhibit Mourning a President. (Both, Donald Hughes.)

Upon arrival at the Capitol, Jackie and her children took a position at the foot of the 36-step entry to the rotunda. There they paused as the Air Force Band played ruffles and flourishes, followed by "Hail to the Chief." Overcome, Jackie lowered her head, and ever so briefly, she wept. They followed the coffin up the steps, where it was placed on the catafalque. Sen. Mike Mansfield, Chief Justice Earl Warren, and Speaker of the House John McCormack all spoke. When the ceremony concluded, Jackie took Caroline by the hand and led her to the bier. As Jackie kissed the flag, Caroline reached under it to touch her father's coffin and touched the heart of the nation. (Right, JFK Library; below, Rowe.)

The rotunda was open to the public, with lines growing throughout the day. Ultimately, attendees would snake three miles through the streets of the nation's capital. Thousands stood in line for hours knowing they would not reach the Capitol in time. The original plan called for the rotunda to be closed at 9:00 p.m. on Sunday night; however, it was kept open throughout the night. Jackie and Robert Kennedy made two separate visits throughout the day and night. When leaving the Capitol, Jackie saw a woman weeping. She walked up to her, and the two embraced. No words were exchanged. On Monday morning, November 25, Jackie returned with Robert and Edward Kennedy, beginning the first part of the funeral ceremonies. (Both, JFK Library.)

The caisson then made its way back down Constitution Avenue to the White House. A cordon of 300 troops from each service branch lined the street. The caisson was followed by President Kennedy's personal flag, carried by Navy seaman E. Nemuth. Some 300,000 citizens lined the road from the White House to the Capitol, and 500,000-plus walked pass President Kennedy's coffin during the 17 hours and 21 minutes he lay in state. (JFK Library.)

Emperors, kings, queens, princes, prime ministers, and delegates from nearly 100 nations arrived in Washington for Monday's funeral. Here, they await the caisson and to be led by Jackie Kennedy to St. Matthew's Cathedral. In front is Pfc. Arthur Carlson and Black Jack, the caparisoned horse. Referencing Black Jack's restlessness throughout the processions, Chapin High senior Diana Carulli called Black Jack "the wild eyed demon follower of death's course . . . the Follower of Death." (Stoughton.)

The FBI, the Secret Service, and the military did all it could to keep Jackie from walking behind her husband's caisson. She walked, "Majestic in her sorrow . . . composed and dignified. . . . With serenity and heroic poise . . . as regal as any emperor, queen or prince who followed her." In *London's Evening Standard*, Lady Jeanne Campbell wrote Jackie had "given the American people from this day on, the one thing they've always lacked, majesty." (JFK Library.)

Jackie (black-veiled) stands between Robert Kennedy (left) and Edward Kennedy, behind Black Jack as they lead the procession of world leaders to St. Matthew's Cathedral. Despite enormous pressure from several fronts, Jackie chose the antiquated St. Matthew's Cathedral over the Shrine of the Immaculate Conception. Her reason was simple: It was where she and her family attended church while they lived in the White House. (Stoughton or Knudsen.)

Cardinal Cushing greets the coffin at St. Matthews. Behind him (in red caps) are Auxiliary Bishop Philip Hannan (left) and Archbishop Patrick O'Boyle (right), of Washington. When Jackie let it be known that she wanted Hannan to deliver the eulogy, a hue and cry went up within the church hierarchy, for he was only an auxiliary bishop. Jackie's response to Sargent Shriver was "Tell them I'm hysterical . . . it has to be Hannan." (Stoughton.)

In a profoundly poignant moment, Jacqueline Kennedy, her children, and members of the Kennedy family watch as President Kennedy's coffin is returned to its caisson. This came following his funeral mass at St. Matthew's Cathedral and began the three-mile final journey to Arlington, where he was laid to rest. (Rowe.)

With the coffin in place, Jackie leaned over and whispered in her son's ear, "It's time to say goodbye to daddy." John F. Kennedy Jr. handed his booklet to his mother, turned, and saluted his father's flag-draped coffin, creating an iconic moment in American history. It was his third birthday. (Stan Stearns.)

Residents of Dallas and nearby communities poured into Dealey Plaza and flooded it with floral tributes. Dallas resident Amy Cunningham, a high school student in 1963, remembered, "For months, possibly years, there were flowers in Dealey Plaza from the people of Dallas." Floral bouquets dominated the landscape for three months, after which the flowers stopped, yet people kept coming, and they continue to do so. (George Reid Collection, the Sixth Floor Museum at Dealey Plaza.)

Old Guard horses Skyline, Count Chris, Blue Dare, Blue, Capp, and Cloud pull the caisson bearing the coffin of JFK over the Memorial Bridge to Arlington. Big Boy carries the section chief, and Black Jack pulls up the rear. A sailor salutes his fallen commander in chief. (Minaud Collection, Sixth Floor Museum at Dealey Plaza.)

The Old Guard Fife and Drum Corps greets the caisson as it makes its entrance into Arlington. Formed in February 1960, the group recalls the days of Washington's Continental army. The uniforms date to about 1781 and consist of black tricorn hats, white wigs, waistcoats, colonial coveralls, and red regimental coats. The musical instruments consist of 10-hole fifes, handmade rope-tensioned drums, and single-valve bugles. They marched in JFK's inaugural parade. (Stoughton.)

Following a 50-jet flyover, one for each state of the Union, Air Force One flew over and dipped its wings. The honor guard then lifted and pulled taut the flag as Cardinal Cushing began to pray. He referred to the president as "our beloved 'Jack' Kennedy, 35th president of the United States." While praying the "Our Father," he came forward and blessed the grave. (US Army/JFK Library.)

Prayers complete, Maj. Stanley Converse of the Army Corps of Engineers handed Jackie a burning wick, which she used to ignite the eternal flame. She then handed the wick to Bobby, who handed it to Ted, as the brothers symbolically placed the wick in the already burning flame. The flag was then folded and handed to Jackie, who departed the hillside. (Rowe.)

Five

THE ETERNAL FLAME

The tradition of the eternal flame dates back to approximately 500 BC and the First Persian Empire. Throughout history, religions, cultures, and nations have utilized the eternal flame to commemorate, memorialize, and honor significant events and individuals. A symbol of enduring ideals, they serve to galvanize and perpetuate the values of a society and its culture, becoming chains in the link of what Abraham Lincoln called "the mystic chords of memory."

John F. Kennedy's legacy was set in motion within hours after his death, and the vehicle to begin its shaping would be his funeral and burial. The chief architect of those events was his 34-year-old widow, First Lady Jacqueline Kennedy. The courage, dignity, and strength she displayed throughout those four heartbreaking days unified the nation, bestowing majesty upon the horror and grief. The day following the assassination, Jackie visited Arlington to approve the gravesite and then returned to the White House and closed herself off in the family quarters upstairs. With her were her brothers-in-law Robert Kennedy and Sargent Shriver and Kennedy aides McGeorge Bundy and Ted Sorenson. They were selecting readings for Monday's funeral. In the midst of the process, Jackie simply uttered, "And there's going to be an eternal flame."

At the time, there were four eternal flames in the United States: the peace memorial dedicated at Gettysburg by Franklin Roosevelt in 1938; the Eternal Flame of the Cherokee Nation; the Tomb of the Unknown Revolutionary War Soldier in Philadelphia, dedicated in 1957; and the Torch of Friendship in Miami, dedicated in 1960. The Torch of Friendship was to light a passageway for immigrants coming from Latin America and the Caribbean and was inspired by the mass fleeing of Cubans seeking asylum following Fidel Castro's ascension as Cuban dictator. In 1964, the torch was rededicated in memory of John F. Kennedy.

On November 22, 1964, an eternal flame was lit at Forest Park in Springfield, Massachusetts, and since that day, an annual service is held each year honoring the late president. In the Mateh Yehuda region near Jerusalem, on July 4, 1966, an eternal flame memorial was dedicated to President Kennedy. The flame is encircled with 51 (representing 50 states and Washington, DC) 60-foot columns. Yad Kennedy is part of the John F. Kennedy Peace Forest. In May 2013, a torch was lit from the eternal flame burning over JFK's grave in Arlington. The torch was then carried to Ireland, where, on June 18, 2013, it was used to light an eternal flame at the dedication of John F. Kennedy Memorial Park in County Wexford, from where JFK's paternal great-grandfather emigrated in 1847. It burns at a monument dedicated to Irish emigrants.

Since Jackie Kennedy lit the flame on the day of her husband's burial, the flame has gone out twice. The first was just weeks after it was lit when a group of Catholic schoolchildren visited and sprinkled holy water on JFK's grave, and the second time was in 1967, shortly after the transfer to a permanent grave. Inclement weather snuffed it out. Since November 25, 1963, the flame has burned, an emblazing symbol of "the energy, the faith, the devotion" John F. Kennedy brought to his presidency.

James Longmore, a World War II Army photographer in Germany, attended the funeral with his wife and five-month-old daughter Ann. As the caisson passed by them, he raised his daughter high, wanting her to "witness history." That afternoon, the Longmores went to Arlington and were among the first citizens to pay respects to the fallen president. The day after the funeral, the newlywed Renauds also visited Arlington and were among the first to view the president's grave on the first day of its official opening. The Longmores and Renauds were among the million people who lined the streets of Washington, DC, to witness the funeral cortege of President Kennedy. (Above, James A. Longmore from the collection of Ann Longmore-Etheridge; below, the George and Pauline Renaud Collection, the Sixth Floor Museum at Dealey Plaza.)

On Thanksgiving morning, before departing for Hyannis Port, Jackie visited the grave with White House staffers, from left to right, Pierre Salinger, Ken O'Donnell (blocked by Salinger), agent Clint Hill, John McNally, and Larry O'Brien. Jackie's sister Lee Radziwill is behind her. The *St. Petersburg Times* wrote, she "knelt before the grave . . . her eyes glistening. . . . Then suddenly the grief faded . . . tranquility lighted her eyes . . . she smiled faintly . . . rose and left." Plans were already under way for his permanent memorial. (JFK Library.)

The day after Thanksgiving was cloudy and raw. However, when Arlington superintendent John Metzler arrived, a throng awaited before locked gates. Before dusk fell, 40,000 people had filed past the grave. With little protocol in place, people swarmed the hillside. Note the line of people snaking down the road as far as the eye can see. (JFK Library.)

Santa Didn't Mind the Discomfort...In Fact, She Was Thrilled

By BERNICE KEANE

Santa Claus didn't mind the warmth of the hall, the heaviness of the boots, and the discomfort of the "stuffing."

She was so thrilled with the job.

Every other day she was an inmate of the Women's Correctional Institution at Framingham. For this day—the day of the annual fair—she was Santa Claus.

She was transformed by the new red velvet suit; it was her big day.

She had grandeur; she had poise. Standing by the sleigh in the center of the room, she greeted each visiting toddler with a grave handshake and a merry twinkle.

When asked what her childhood Christmases were like and whether she got toys, she said in a soft, even voice,

"We never got a toy."

"Never?" It seemed hard to believe.

"No, never. My father died when I

was two. There were six others. My mother used to sit down before Christmas and explain that we wouldn't get anything."

"Did you believe in Santa?"

"Oh, we believed all right. And we hoped—but he never came."

She said they lived on a small farm and had little else but the most meager food.

Now she was playing the Santa role—and loving every minute.

"They love doing the things they never experienced in childhood," explained a staff member, Mrs. Joyce Temple.

The fair booths abounded in the things of childhood.

Stuffed animals made by the girls, dolls dressed in handmade creations, homemade candies, cakes and ceramics.

GLOBE SANTA
Page 4

Santa's Friends

TO HELP GLOBE SANTA
Send check or money order to
BOX 1825, Boston 6, Mass., or
visit Santa's Headquarters at
319 Washington st.

FRIENDS
Page 5

The Boston Globe

MORNING EDITION

THURSDAY, DECEMBER 5, 1963

Telephone AV 8-5000   56 PAGES—10c

GUIDE TO FEATURES

SEASONED REASON

THURSDAY — Some clouds, cold.
FRIDAY—Still cold.

Kennedy Babies Reburied With Him

Bodies of Patrick Bouvier and Infant Girl Removed to Arlington

By WILFRID C. RODGERS
(Washington Correspondent)
Copyright, 1963, Globe Newspaper Co.

WASHINGTON—Two children of President and Mrs. John F. Kennedy who died at or soon after birth were quietly moved to Arlington National Cemetery Wednesday to rest beside their father.

This was done in accordance with the wishes of the President's wife, Mrs. Jacqueline Kennedy. She said it was what he would have wanted.

The body of Patrick Bouvier Kennedy, who died last Aug. 7, only 48 hours after birth, was

1956, had been buried at Newport, R.I., the home of Mrs. Kennedy's mother.

The transfer of the bodies had been painstakingly planned in advance to insure secrecy and avoid any semblance of a spectacle.

The plan was carried out so successfully that the public was unaware of what had transpired until after the infants were buried Wednesday night.

Richard Cardinal Cushing and Judge Francis X. Morrissey of Boston, both old friends of the Kennedy family, accompanied Patrick's body to Quonset, R.I. They were unnoticed as they drove from Brookline to Rhode Island in the funeral director's car.

Quonset. He attracted no notice there and flew back to Washington aboard the Caroline with the two caskets.

The Globe learned Wednesday morning of the plan, but kept the secret in accordance with the wishes of the family.

Wednesday night they were laid to rest, one on either side of their father, on a grassy slope overlooking the Potomac River where he himself was buried only eight days ago.

The burial was carried out in complete privacy. Only Mrs. Kennedy and eight other persons, five of them members of the family, were present.

Simple services, lasting but 20 minutes, were

How Jacqueline remembers the tragic day . . . Page 56.

It was Mrs. Kennedy's express wish that the disinterment and transfer of the two tiny bodies be accomplished absolutely without public notice.

And so it was done. Even some members of the Kennedy family did not know about it until afterwards.

The first public announcement was made after the graveside services at 9 p.m.

With Mrs. Kennedy were her sister, Princess Lee Radziwill; Patricia Lawford, the President's sister; his brothers, Atty. Gen. Robert F. Kennedy

On December 4, Kennedy family friends Frank Morrissey and Richard Cardinal Cushing accompanied the exhumed coffin of Patrick to the tarmac at Quonset Navy Base in Rhode Island. There, they met Jackie's mother, Janet Auchincloss, who had accompanied the exhumed coffin of JFK and Jackie's stillborn baby girl, who was buried in St. Columba's Cemetery in Middleton, Rhode Island. The coffins were placed on the Kennedy family plane, the *Caroline*, and they were accompanied by Sen. Ted Kennedy to Washington, where they were placed in two separate Army trucks and driven to Arlington. At 8:45 p.m., Jackie arrived at Arlington, and in a 10-minute ceremony officiated by Bishop Phillip Hannan, the babies were laid to rest beside their father. At the ceremony were Jackie, Ted, Bobby Kennedy, Lee Radziwill, Patricia Kennedy Lawford, and Ted's wife, Joan. (Above, AC; below, JFK Library.)

The internment of the children next to their father fulfilled Jackie's pledge to "bring them together." Patrick's stone reads, "Patrick Bouvier Kennedy, Aug 7, 1963–Aug 9, 1963." The cross upon the grave of the stillborn girl, whom they would have called Arabella, reads "Baby Girl Kennedy, August 23, 1956." On the base of the cross is engraved, "Suffer Little Children to Come unto Me." Three different United Press International (UPI) reports in December stated 500,000 to a million visitors (16,000–32,000 per day) had made their pilgrimage to the grave. Below, note the line winding way down the road—a commonplace scene. Both photographs were taken in December 1963. (Above, Azina Smart; below, Edward Crellin Collection.)

Snow fell upon the grave just before Christmas. C. Henry King, a journalist with North Carolina's *High Point Enterprise*, visited. He wrote of the 40,000 daily visitors, "The air of respect was so intense that one could sense that these gatherers came not as the curious of sightseers . . . but as humble citizens to pay their respects, to show deference, and perhaps to subliminally murmur 'I'm sorry' to lighten hearts still heavy within them." (Andrew Endres.)

Texas governor John Connolly and his wife, Nellie, visited JFK's grave on February 28, 1964. Connolly's right wrist remains in a cast, broken by a bullet that struck him in the shooting that killed JFK. Nellie places a bouquet of yellow roses upon the grave. JFK's last words were spoken to Nellie Connolly and, ironically, were in response to her observation of how wonderful was their reception in Dallas. (JFK Library.)

The coming of spring ignited an explosion of visitors to JFK's grave. Arlington superintendent John Metzler said, "It's more than we could possibly conceive." On Easter Sunday, it took the line an hour and a half to move up the hill to the graveside. Newspapers across the country reported, "They used to come by the thousands, now they come by the tens of thousands." (Photograph by Matt Bumgardner.)

On the morning of May 28, 1964, Pres. Lyndon Johnson presided over a 10-minute memorial service in the White House State Dining Room, honoring President Kennedy. Quoting scripture, he said of Kennedy that he was "one of those that were honored in their generations and were the glory of their times." He then visited Arlington, where he laid a wreath at the grave. Behind him are Lady Bird Johnson and Gen. Chester Clifton. (JFK Library.)

May 29 marked what would have been JFK's 47th birthday. That morning, the Kennedy family attended mass at St. Matthew's Cathedral and then made their way to Arlington to visit the grave. At left, Jackie approaches the grave entrance with John and Caroline (partially blocked) in hand. At far right is Attorney General Robert Kennedy, and at far left is his wife, Ethel. Below, they approached the grave, where they knelt and prayed. John then took off his PT-109 tie clasp and placed it under the flowers his mother left. That evening from the Kennedy Compound in Hyannis, Jackie and Robert were interviewed on CBS in a worldwide broadcast event, within which Jackie said most important was her husband's "desire to inspire people to take an active part in the life of their country." (Both photographs by Matt Bumgardner.)

This was the look of the temporary grave from JFK's internment in November 1963 until his move to the permanent site in March 1967. The summer of 1964 saw an average of 50,000 visitors per day from May 30 through September 7. The Army noted that the visitation peaked the last three weeks of August, amassing 50,000 per day. Five million visitors came the first summer of JFK's internment. (JFK Library.)

Neither rain, snow, sleet, nor cold kept people from paying their respects at the president's grave. Nearly eight million people visited the first year. On the first anniversary of JFK's death, 30,000 people braved 20-degree temperatures to visit his grave. Jackie spent the day secluded at home in New York with her sister Lee Radziwill and Prince Radziwill and Jean Kennedy Smith and her husband, Steven. (JFK Library.)

On January 20, 1965, Lyndon Johnson was inaugurated president, and just as with his predecessor, snow accompanied the event. A steady stream of invited guests made the trip to Arlington to pay their respects to President Kennedy. For Robert Kennedy, newly elected senator from the state of New York, the day was deeply poignant. Kneeling at his brother's eternal flame, he grasped a handful of snow. (JFK Library.)

The first weekend of February 1966 brought a blizzard to the nation's capital. However, it did not keep two unidentified Sisters of St. Joseph from paying their respects at the president's gravesite. The snow covered the entirety of Patrick's stone while the top of Arabella's stone cross remains visible. (JFK Library.)

On May 8, 1965, approximately 500 Holocaust survivors made a pilgrimage of thanksgiving to Washington, DC, to celebrate the 20th anniversary of the Nazi surrender (VE Day). Their first stop was JFK's grave. They were met by six picketing members of the American Nazi Party. Sen. Robert Kennedy had forewarned them, stating, "America even has room for the . . . slightly mad . . . slightly demented," and he urged them to ignore them, which they did. (JFK Library.)

Carol Harding was a 10-year-old fifth grade student in Maryland when JFK was assassinated. In the summer of 1965, her family made the pilgrimage that millions of Americans were making to visit the fallen president's grave. The summers following the president's death would find approximately 50,000 people a day waiting up to an hour, and sometimes more, to pass by the grave. (Jack Martin.)

The first soil testing for the permanent gravesite took place at the end of November 1964, and on September 6, the land began to be cleared, as seen here. The initial completion date of the construction was targeted for some time in the fall of 1966. (JFK Library.)

On April 11, 1966, the first granite stone was placed at the permanent gravesite. It came from the Deer Island Granite Company in Stonington, Maine. Twelve feet long and weighing eleven tons, this was the first of over 2,000 slabs, which would comprise the final memorial gravesite. (JFK Library.)

In June 1966, John Benson, a stonecutter from Newport, Rhode Island, paints the words of JFK's inaugural address at the new gravesite. After painting, he chiseled them into permanence into the 12-ton granite block. As his father had before him, Benson owned the John Stevens Shop, which was founded in 1705. John's son Nick is the third-generation owner of the Stevens Shop. (JFK Library.)

In the late summer of 1966, Carol Harding's family returned to Arlington, which now featured a far different look than the previous summer, as the new memorial and gravesite took shape. Note the lower right-hand corner where people are visiting the president's temporary site and John Benson's shaded workspace (center). (Jack Martin.)

A soldier stands at the ready in the fall of 1966 as work proceeds on the permanent gravesite behind him. The members of the Old Guard who watched over JFK and brought him to his rest in 1963 stood watch over his entire time in the temporary grave. From 7:30 a.m. until 7:00 p.m., two stood watch, and one stood watch through the night. (JFK Library.)

Fall gave way to winter, and in early 1967, the memorial neared completion. Snow brought setbacks, but as winter gave way to spring, the final resting place for President Kennedy and his two infant children was ready. Just days short of the spring solstice, workers, officials, and Robert and Edward Kennedy, along with Boston's archbishop Richard Cardinal Cushing, gathered on the hillside to lay John F. Kennedy to rest. (JFK Library.)

Six

WITH YOUR TINY INFANTS BY YOUR SIDE

As night fell on the evening of March 14, 1967, approximately 250 soldiers moved into place in a ring formation around the entrance to Arlington National Cemetery. Their purpose was to seal off the entry gate. On Arlington's hillside, workers were in place to transfer the remains of John F. Kennedy and two of his children to their permanent resting place.

A press release by the Department of Defense dated March 15, 1967, read in part, "The reinternment began at 6:19 and was completed at 9:02 p.m. . . . Other work at the gravesite continued through the night. . . . Some landscaping remains. . . . But President Kennedy's permanent grave . . . is open to visits by the public."

The previous week, Cardinal Cushing received a phone call from Ted Kennedy, asking him to officiate at the gravesite. The 72-year-old prelate and longtime family friend arrived the night before and stood with Ted and Bobby Kennedy through the reinternments. He returned to conduct the services at the new gravesites at 7:00 a.m. the following morning.

A raw rain fell throughout the 20-minute service as members of the Kennedy family gathered. Reports circulated that it was the first known gravesite visit by Jacqueline Kennedy since May 29, 1964, when she took her children there commemorating the 47th birthday of their father.

The Army band played the national anthem, the Navy Hymn, and "The Boys of Wexford," linking this country with the country of JFK's ancestors. "The Boys of Wexford" is about Ireland's fight for independence, specifically the Irish Rebellion of 1798. Visiting Ireland in June 1963, a choir of 600 students sang "The Boys of Wexford" to JFK. When asked if he would like to hear another song, he replied, "Another verse of 'The Boys of Wexford' would be fine." He then joined the chorus, singing along with the students. Returning to the United States, the president asked the Marine Band to compose an arrangement of the song, which was played at his graveside on this rainy morn. Cardinal Cushing then prayed:

> The eyes of the world have turned many times to this hillside to freshen the memory of youth and life which all of us knew such a little while ago. . . . Generations will journey here to be close to his greatness which once we knew and so recently have lost.
>
> Dear God, our Heavenly Father, look down upon this hallowed place, reach out your love to John Fitzgerald Kennedy, cover him with your mercy and give him joy eternal with your saints. . . . Bless O Lord, the loved ones who are here today. . . . Replace with your grace the empty loss that they have known, the vacant chair, the silent voice and the lonely night. . . . Watch over the country that we love. . . . Make us strong in virtue and bold in the service of our fellow man. Teach us to cherish liberty and use it wisely, to put our feet in . . . the footprints which he bequeathed to us. . . . Be at peace dear Jack with your tiny infants by your side, until we all meet again above this hill and beyond the stars.

At 6:19 p.m. on March 14, 1967, under the cover of darkness, work commenced disinterring the bodies of John F. Kennedy, his son Patrick, and his stillborn baby girl, who would have been named Arabella. The new graves sit open and waiting; a new flame was ignited with a torch, lit from the original flame. (Stoughton.)

The unearthing begins. Present, among others, were Robert Kennedy; Edward Kennedy; Cardinal Richard Cushing; Secretary of Defense Robert McNamara; Paul C. Warnke, general counsel for the Department of Defense; Alfred B. Fitt, general counsel for the Department of the Army; and John Metzler, superintendent of Arlington National Cemetery. (Stoughton.)

The first vault to be uncovered was that of Patrick Bouvier Kennedy, and it was placed in its permanent grave at 7:07 p.m. Patrick was born five-weeks premature on August 7, 1963, and lived only 39 hours before succumbing to Hyaline Membrane Disease, a lung affliction. He preceded his father in death by 104 days, and he was laid to rest at his side in the temporary grave on December 6, 1963. (Both, Stoughton.)

President Kennedy's vault sits in the temporary grave on the right. On the left is a metal box containing the remains of Arabella, a stillborn baby girl, birthed on August 23, 1956. The metal box was placed in its own vault, below. (Both, Stoughton.)

Arabella's vault was larger than anticipated, requiring more work to be done on her permanent grave. Simultaneously workers continued on freeing the president's vault. With that accomplished, Robert Kennedy watches transfixed as the crane hook begins to lift his brother's vault. (Both, Stoughton.)

Robert Kennedy follows the vault of their brother as Edward Kennedy (at right, arms folded) watches while workers guide the casket toward its permanent resting place. (Stoughton.)

At 8:21 p.m., President Kennedy's vault was lowered into its permanent grave. Edward and Robert Kennedy look on contemplatively while Cardinal Cushing rubs his brow. (Stoughton.)

The *Boston Globe* of March 16, 1967, reported the words of Cardinal Cushing: "It was a pretty sad affair. . . . They were reliving this whole tragedy, especially Bob, standing over the grave, looking into it." Edward Kennedy would relive this scenario on the night of November 30, 1971. That night, he and Bobby's widow, Ethel, arrived at Arlington after the gates were closed, and for three hours, they stood vigil while Bobby's casket was disinterred and reburied 100 feet farther down Arlington's grassy hillside. His final resting place is 125 feet from President Kennedy's. (Both, Stoughton.)

With President Kennedy's vault in place, the crane hook guided the vault of Arabella to her final rest at the left hand of her father. She was placed in her grave at 8:26 p.m. Robert and Edward Kennedy observe, and Cardinal Cushing wipes a tear from his eye. It was Robert Kennedy who stood at her graveside in St. Columba's Cemetery in Middleton, Rhode Island, when she was buried in August 1956. (Stoughton.)

With all of the vaults in place, Cardinal Cushing stood over them and offered a prayer: "Be at peace dear Jack, with your tiny infants at your side. Until we all meet again above this hill and beyond the stars." (Stoughton.)

Robert Kennedy stands over the partially buried vault of his brother as workers cover it. (Stoughton.)

It took only 36 minutes to bury the vaults, and at 9:02 p.m., the task was complete. The entire process took two hours and forty-three minutes. Family members left while workers toiled through the night to prepare for the 7:00 a.m. ceremony the following morning. (Stoughton.)

Cardinal Cushing leads the prayers bringing the brief ceremony to a close. It was a quiet, somber ceremony, in which the cardinal said, "Hardly a word was exchanged among those present." Most present were family members along with friends Kenny O'Donnell and Ben Smith, who was appointed by Kennedy to fill his vacant Senate seat after his election as president. President Johnson was among the guests as well. (Stoughton.)

On Saturday afternoon, November 23, 1963, Jackie visited this same hillside in Arlington to give the final approval of the final resting place for her husband. A chilling, soaking rain was falling, leaving the hillside soft and sloshy. That chilling rain returned in March 1967 as, once again, Jacqueline Kennedy returned to the Arlington hillside, leaving a small bouquet of lilies of the valley. (Stoughton.)

Seven

WITH HISTORY THE FINAL JUDGE OF OUR DEEDS

On January 20, 1961, John F. Kennedy was inaugurated the 35th president of the United States. He was the first president born in the 20th century and the youngest man ever elected to the office. He opened his speech invoking his "forbears" and reiterated their belief that "the rights of man come not from the generosity of the state but from the hand of God." Acknowledging the perils of the nuclear age, he declared, "Let the word go forth from this time and place, to friend and foe alike, that the torch has been passed to a new generation of Americans."

He challenged Americans with his "New Frontier," calling it "not a set of promises . . . but a set of challenges." He challenged Americans to join in the "long twilight struggle . . . against the common enemies of man: tyranny, poverty, disease and war itself." He created the Peace Corps, and by the last summer of his life, 5,000 Americans had made the commitment and joined. At the centennial of his birth, over 220,000 Americans had served in the Peace Corps in 140 countries around the globe. He challenged Americans to reach for the stars and set NASA's course for the moon. A decade later, 24 Americans had orbited the moon, and 12 had walked its surface. All "returned safely to earth." He challenged the Soviet Union to "explore what problems unite us instead of belaboring those problems which divide us." In the last summer of his life, the United States and the Soviet Union signed a nuclear test ban treaty, which would one day bear the signatures of 184 nations. He challenged his segregated country saying, "This nation . . . will not be fully free until all its citizens are free. . . . The time has come for this nation to fulfill its promise." In the last summer of his life, he signed the Equal Pay Act to abolish wage disparity based on sex, and he sent a civil rights package to Congress, which ultimately became the 1964 Civil Rights Act.

In June 1963, President Kennedy, speaking at the American University's commencement, talked of his world vision: "What kind of peace do I mean? What kind of peace do we seek? . . . The kind of peace that makes life on earth worth living, the kind that enables men and nations to grow and to hope and to build a better life for their children—not merely peace for Americans but peace for all men and women—not merely peace in our time but peace for all time."

Eighteenth-century English poet Alexander Pope wrote, "Hope springs eternal in the human breast." On a hillside in Arlington, a flickering flame, lit by a courageous young widow, serves as an eternal reminder of that hope.

Four million people come every year. In a steady stream, they walk the granite steps past the signs imploring silence and respect. They pause, reach for their phones, and photograph the flickering flame. Baby boomers often linger a bit longer, reading his words as they gaze upon the bridge that bore his caisson. They hear his voice, and they remember, like a 66-year-old retired history teacher who was an elementary school student when John and Jacqueline Kennedy lived at 1600 Pennsylvania Avenue. "He made me feel like my life could make a difference," he recalled. Then he sighed and said simply, "I hope it has."

Taken shortly after the transfer, this image shows the unfinished landscaping. Note the military hats surrounding the eternal flame. They sat atop the temporary grave starting in November 1963, when JFK was buried, and were removed permanently on April 18, 1967. Many letters were written lauding the gesture that led them there, but it detracted from the simplicity and beauty of the grave. The Department of Defense concurred. (JFK Library.)

In this image, taken in September 1967, two months after the completion of the landscaping, a member of the Old Guard stands watch. On January 11, 1971, the Department of the Army announced, "Effective 1700 (5:00 p.m.) 14, February, 1971, the third infantry detail at the Kennedy gravesite will be discontinued." The following morning at 8:00 a.m., the security forces of Arlington took over the functions of the detail. (US Army/ Carl Schneider.)

Robert F. Kennedy was a frequent visitor to his brother's grave, often leaping the wall late at night or predawn. In June 1968, he too fell to an assassin's bullet following his victory in the California Democratic primary, and he joined his brother in rest on the same Arlington hillside. Seen above is his original gravesite high on the hill. In November 1971, he was moved 100 feet down the hill upon completion of his memorial. A 1968 Christmas card carried the following message: "In Arlington lie two brothers, two patriots, two Americans; who had compassion and love for their fellowman and God. There is peace in Arlington Cemetery and those there are close to God. But Dear Lord when will we have peace on earth and goodwill toward men for always? Marylea." (Both, JFK Library.)

Ted Kennedy casts a wistful glance at brother Robert's grave while other family members turn toward the fountain memorial. He often visited both graves, and as the 10th anniversary of JFK's death was approaching, over 40 million visitors had paid their respects at JFK's grave. The summer following Bobby's death, it was reported that 100,000 a day made pilgrimages to Arlington. (JFK Library.)

This photograph was taken in the summer of 1992, twenty-five years after the transfer to the final graves. The moss grows thick between the granite covering the graves, and the landscaping has flourished, both fulfilling the intent of the initial design. (RPS.)

On May 19, 1994, Jacqueline Bouvier Kennedy Onassis died of complications from non-Hodgkin's lymphoma. She was two months short of her 65th birthday. Five days later, she returned to Arlington for the final time and was laid to rest next to her husband and children on the hillside she had chosen and beneath the flame she had lit. (AC.)

Sargent Shriver visits the gravesite around 2000. A World War II Navy veteran, Shriver married Eunice Kennedy in 1953. The first director of the Peace Corps, it was Shriver who executed Jackie's wishes for JFK's funeral. He died in 2011 following an eight-year battle with Alzheimer's disease. Peace Corps director Aaron Williams stated Shriver "served as our founder, friend, and guiding light for the past 50 years . . . his legacy . . . will live on in the work of current and future Peace Corps volunteers." (JFK Library.)

In August 2009, Sen. Edward Kennedy died of brain cancer. He was buried 100 feet south of his brother Robert (two white crosses), whose grave is 125 south of the graves of JFK and his family. Immediately, work began on the walkway connecting all the graves. It was completed in 2012 with the addition of the cenotaph of Joseph P. Kennedy Jr., who was killed in World War II; his body was never recovered. (RPS.)

This photograph was taken just before spring in March 2013 before the fescue and clover between the stones had turned to summer green. The vibrant red and brown hues provide an unusual look of the gravesite, one which is rarely seen. (Ron Cogswell.)

On April 29, 2013, JFK's grave was prepared for repairs to the eternal flame. First, a temporary white fence was constructed to seal off the gravestones from the flame repair. Engineering technician Randy Barton then lit a torch from the eternal flame, which was then used to light a temporary burner while the permanent flame was repaired and upgraded. The process was then reversed when work was completed in time for JFK's birthday. (US Army/Patrick Bloodgood.)

Lyndsey Tyler visited the gravesite Memorial Day weekend 2013, which also happened to be two days before JFK's 96th birthday celebration. She found the grave covered in a beautiful array of roses and American flags. (Lyndsey Tyler.)

In May 1964, Lyndon Johnson laid a wreath at JFK's grave commemorating his 47th birthday. The following two years, on JFK's birthday, he sent a military envoy to lay flowers on his behalf. In 1967, he extended that gesture to include the birthdays of all deceased presidents, beginning a tradition that is carried on today. This photograph was taken during the ceremony commemorating JFK's 97th birthday in 2014. (Department of Defense/EJ Herson.)

In 1961, President Kennedy authorized the "green beret" as the official headgear for all US Army Special Forces. On the day of the president's funeral, Sgt. Maj. Francis Ruddy removed his own green beret and placed it upon the grave of his commander in chief. Each year, the Green Berets lay a wreath at the grave. This was the ceremony in October 2015. (US Army/Rachel Larue/ Arlington National Cemetery.)

On November 22, 1964, Hugh Milligan wrote in the *St. Louis Dispatch*: "Since he was laid to rest, he's never been alone. . . . Day or night, winter or summer, someone always comes. . . . No matter what the weather, someone always comes." It was true then and it is true today—even a chilly raw December rain does not keep people away. (RPS.)

Pictured is the grave as it looked in 2017, JFK's 100th birthday year. To the right of the Lincoln Memorial are the Washington Monument, the Capitol dome, and the Jefferson Memorial. The eternal flame sits on the axis point connecting with the Custis-Lee Mansion, Arlington's entry gate, the approach to Arlington, the Memorial Bridge, and the Lincoln Memorial. It is from this view that JFK commented, "I could stay here forever." (RPS.)

Fire and light were an underlying theme throughout John F. Kennedy's inaugural address and a prelude to the signet of his speech, when within its conclusion he said, "The energy, the faith, the devotion which we bring to this endeavor will light our country and all who serve it—and the glow from that fire can truly light the world. And so, my fellow Americans: ask not what your country can do for you—ask what you can do for your country." On November 23, 1963, Jacqueline Kennedy, numb with grief and awash in sorrow, let it be known that an eternal flame would burn upon his grave. Decades roll by, time marches on, and Cardinal Cushing's words have proved prophetic; for "generations have journeyed to Arlington's hillside to be close to his greatness." (Both, US Army/Rachel Larue/Arlington National Cemetery.)

ABOUT THE ORGANIZATION

The Sixth Floor Museum at Dealey Plaza chronicles the assassination and legacy of Pres. John F. Kennedy, interprets the Dealey Plaza National Historic Landmark District and the John F. Kennedy Memorial Plaza, and presents contemporary culture within the context of presidential history. Its vision is to be an impartial, multigenerational destination and forum for exploring the memory and effects of the events surrounding the assassination of President Kennedy through sharing his legacy and its impact on an ever-changing global society.

Over 400,000 people a year visit from all over the world as an ongoing testament to the enduring legacy of John F. Kennedy.

DISCOVER THOUSANDS OF LOCAL HISTORY BOOKS
FEATURING MILLIONS OF VINTAGE IMAGES

Arcadia Publishing, the leading local history publisher in the United States, is committed to making history accessible and meaningful through publishing books that celebrate and preserve the heritage of America's people and places.

Find more books like this at
www.arcadiapublishing.com

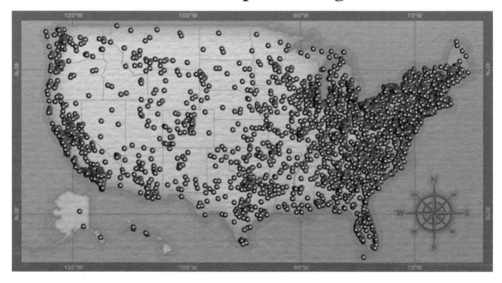

Search for your hometown history, your old stomping grounds, and even your favorite sports team.

Consistent with our mission to preserve history on a local level, this book was printed in South Carolina on American-made paper and manufactured entirely in the United States. Products carrying the accredited Forest Stewardship Council (FSC) label are printed on 100 percent FSC-certified paper.

MADE IN THE